# A MILITARY FORCE FOR A GLOBALLY ENGAGED SUPER POWER

by

Lieutenant Colonel Andrew J. Kostic
United States Marine Corps

Colonel David A. Kelley
Project Adviser

This SRP is submitted in partial fulfillment of the requirements of the Master of Strategic Studies Degree. The U.S. Army War College is accredited by the Commission on Higher Education of the Middle States Association of Colleges and Schools, 3624 Market Street, Philadelphia, PA 19104, (215) 662-5606. The Commission on Higher Education is an institutional accrediting agency recognized by the U.S. Secretary of Education and the Council for Higher Education Accreditation.

U.S. Army War College
CARLISLE BARRACKS, PENNSYLVANIA 17013

# ABSTRACT

AUTHOR:            Lieutenant Colonel Andrew J. Kostic

TITLE:              A Military Force for a Globally Engaged Super Power

FORMAT:          Strategy Research Project

DATE:              1 March 2010      WORD COUNT: 6,558      PAGES: 34

KEY TERMS:     Marine Corps, Amphibious, Expeditionary

CLASSIFICATION: Unclassified

For decades the United States organized, equipped and trained its military forces to defeat the conventional military forces of the Soviet Union. The world changed overnight with the fall of the Soviet Union and so did the United States' adversaries. Terrorists and religious extremists are the new threat to the United States. The Department of Defense continues to evaluate the type of military forces required to combat this emerging global threat and execute the National Security Strategy. As the United States Army undergoes transformation from a Division centric, armor heavy organization to a lighter, expeditionary Brigade Combat Team structure, this paper proposes that the Army needs to maintain the conventional combat capabilities it perfected during the Cold War, and that the Marine Corps, with its expeditionary nature and amphibious forcible entry capability, is the ideal military force to meet the future strategic needs of the United States to effectively combat rising global threats and to secure America's vital national interests.

# A MILITARY FORCE FOR A GLOBALLY ENGAGED SUPER POWER

Since its foundation, the United States has maintained a military force to defend itself and protect its vital national interests: from the massive armies of the Civil War created to preserve the Union, to the Great White Fleet of the early 1900s created to demonstrate America's military power to the world. The United States' commitment to building and maintaining a military force that could execute its National Security Strategy was instrumental to its rise to super power status with vital national interests worldwide. As the United States continues to expand its influence and looks to define future adversaries and ways to combat them, this paper suggests the United States Marine Corps is the ideal military force to support the National Security Strategy of a globally engaged super power.

## Cold War National Security Strategy

From 1945 until the end of the Cold War, the most significant threat to the United States' vital national interests was the Soviet Union and communism. The strategy the United States vigorously pursued for more than 40 years to counter this threat was one of containment.[1] This required the United States to maintain a strong military posture and resulted in a robust Cold War conventional military force which never fell below 2 million active duty personnel and peaked at over 3.5 million.[2] This force was strategically positioned throughout the world in an effort to prevent the spread of communism and to halt a Soviet attack across Europe.

To counter the Soviet Union's build up of nuclear weapons and deter them from using their weapons against the United States or its allies, the United States constructed a massive nuclear arsenal of its own. By the end of the Cold War, the

United States possessed some 23,000 nuclear weapons while the Soviet Union had amassed an estimated 27,000 nuclear weapons.[3]

Fully dedicated to its National Security Strategy, the United States fought two regional conflicts in an effort to contain communism and curtail the expansion of the Soviet empire, one in Korea and the other in Vietnam. These two conflicts cost the lives of more than 94,000 Americans.[4] However, the United States' steadfast commitment to its strategy of containment prevailed, and the Soviet Union collapsed. At the end of the Cold War, the United States emerged as the world's predominant super power.

A Global National Security Strategy

Following the Cold War, the United States rejected the idea of isolationism and recommitted itself to being a global leader in a new unipolar world. In 2006, President George W. Bush founded the National Security Strategy upon leading a growing global community of democracies to end tyranny throughout the world by "promoting freedom, justice, and human dignity" and by extending "prosperity through free and fair trade and wise development of policies."[5] This strategy expounded that to achieve long-term security the United States must commit itself to aid in the development of well-governed democratic states throughout the world that can provide for the basic needs of their people and be responsible members of the international community.[6] Some of the essential tasks to promote this strategy included "strengthening alliances to defeat global terrorism, defusing regional conflicts, igniting a new era of global economic growth, developing agendas for cooperative action with other centers of global power, and transforming America's national security institutions to meet the challenges and opportunities of the 21st century."[7] All of these tasks have direct implications for the U.S. Department of Defense and its strategic outlook on defending the Nation.

The National Defense Strategy is aligned to support the National Security Strategy and places special emphasis on defending the homeland, promoting security, and deterring conflicts.[8] The most important responsibility of any government is to provide for the security of its people. As a global super power, the security of the United States is intricately linked with the security of the international system. There are four key elements to the United States' National Defense Strategy which directly relate to the international arena: ensuring the security of the global commons for all; strengthening and expanding alliances and partnerships; enhancing global security and preventing conflict; and balancing military forces and capabilities to be able to respond to threats across the range of military operations.[9]

The global commons provide access to the world's markets and resources. Ensuring their security and safe use by all nations allows for the expansion of global economic growth. In addition, using security cooperation activities to assist other countries in improving their military capabilities to combat insurgencies, terrorism, proliferations, and other threats not only strengthens U.S. alliances and partnerships, but also enhances global security.

However, the most effective way to enhance global security and prevent conflict is through deterrence. Maintaining a credible military capability is essential to deter potential adversaries and reassure the American people and their allies of the United States' commitment to defend them. The challenges of deterrence have direct ties with those of balancing military forces and capabilities to be able to respond to threats across the range of military operations while simultaneously transforming the United States overseas military presence to a more agile, continental U.S. based expeditionary force. In the midst of global changes and challenges, the United States Marine Corps serves as a model force for executing the National Defense Strategy in today's strategic operating environment.

## Strategic Operating Environment

The world's vast expanses of water play a significant role in the global economy and are one of the focal points of the future strategic operating environment. More than two-thirds of the earth's surface is covered by water. On any given day there are some 23,000 ships underway carrying 90 percent of the world's international commerce across the seas. The political, economic, and social world stays connected via underwater cables which carry 95 percent of the international voice and data communications. Approximately 49 percent of the world's oil travels over water through 6 major chokepoints around the globe, and 23% of the world's oil and gas is drilled at sea.[10] As globalization improves economic development, the world's population centers shift toward the source of economic prosperity, the sea.

The littorals, or coastal regions, are increasingly becoming areas of significant strategic importance. Nearly 75 percent of all people live within 200 miles of the coast.[11] In addition, 80 percent of all countries have borders against the sea and 80 percent of the world's capitals are located within 300 nautical miles of the sea.[12] By the year 2025, it is projected that more than 60 percent of the world's population will reside in urban areas, which indicates that the world will be dominated by urban littorals.[13] The sea commons will continue to be of increasing importance to the future of globalization, and the United States' national security is intimately tied to maintaining stability in the littoral area.

A changing world view of the United States places even more emphasis on the strategic importance of the seas. Foreign sensitivity to U.S. military presence overseas has steadily increased since the end of the Cold War. Even close allies to the United States have become reluctant, for internal or regional political reasons, to allow U.S. military forces on their soil. This was never more evident than in 2003 when Turkey refused to let the U.S. Army 4th Infantry Division stage on its southern border so the United States could open a second front against Iraq during the opening phase of Operation Iraqi Freedom.[14] Diminishing access of U.S. military forces overseas complicates the United States' ability to maintain a forward presence and significantly alters the Department of Defense's strategic requirements. This change in attitude of foreign states requires the United States to place greater emphasis on its maritime capabilities in order to retain freedom of action on the seas and to have unfettered access to strategic regions around the world. Maritime dominance is essential for the United States to secure its vital national interests and counter future threats to its national security.

<u>Future Threats</u>

With the demise of the Soviet Union, the threat the United States faced for over 40 years disappeared almost overnight. However, the period of peace and tranquility was short lived as new threats emerged to challenge western influence and globalization from both state and non-state actors. Violent extremist ideology seeking to overturn the international state system replaced communism in the strategic environment. In addition, North Korea and Iran remain rogue states, founded on tyranny, and continue to pose significant threats to the security of the United States with their proliferation of nuclear weapons. Along with these adversaries, the United States

5

faces three primary challenges to its national security: rising tensions in the sea commons, hybrid threats, and failing states.[15]

The first challenge to the future security of the United States is the sea commons. China continues to grow and enhance its naval capabilities, and its new founded naval nationalism indicates that it will embark on an ambitious maritime policy.[16] However, strong conventional naval forces are not the only source of rising tensions on the water. The primary opposition to open sea lines of communications are asymmetric threats. Iran's armada of fast boats armed with unsophisticated and inexpensive makeshift weaponry pose a viable threat to all ships, combatant and commercial, transiting through the Strait of Hormuz and Persian Gulf.[17] In addition, one of the oldest professions in the world—piracy—has become a very lucrative crime once again. In 2009, over 100 ships were attacked by pirates in the Gulf of Aden alone, with pirates successfully capturing 42 of those vessels.[18] Soaring ship insurance rates and the interruption of the flow of commerce caused by piracy has placed an undue burden on an already fragile global economy.

The second challenge the United States faces are hybrid threats. Hybrid military threats are nothing new. Militaries, resistance fighters, and terrorists have been using both regular and irregular warfare to their advantage for centuries. As recent as the 1970s, the United States was involved in a hybrid conflict in Vietnam, where irregular Vietcong forces operated in unison with regular North Vietnamese military forces to achieve one political objective. However, the cause for concern is that the boundaries between regular and irregular warfare are blurring, with non-state actors acquiring weapons that were once only available to states, and states turning more and more to unconventional strategies to counter the United States overwhelming conventional military power.[19]

Hybrid wars "mix the lethality of state conflict with the fanatical and protracted fervor of irregular warfare."[20] Hezbollah clearly demonstrated the ability of non-state actors to acquire sophisticated anti-tank weapons and to integrate radical militia forces with highly trained fighters and anti-tank guided missiles teams to fight Israel in 2006, and had overwhelming success.[21] Future challenges to the United States' national security will see a mix of military and nonmilitary threats by both states and non-state actors.[22] Some may materialize as specific acts towards the United States or its interests, such as terrorism, insurgency, or strategic criminal activity, while others may not have any anti-U.S. purpose, such as civil war, state failure, and natural or manmade catastrophes.[23]

The third challenge to the future security of the United States likewise poses a serious risk to global security—weak and failing states. Failed states generally emerge as the result of some form of conflict when a government can no longer provide the basic conditions and responsibilities of a sovereign state. With the collapse of a state's criminal justice system, chaos usually ensues and some form of organized crime prevails, leaving the people of the state "susceptible to the exhortation of demagogues and hatemongers."[24] Failed states are excellent breeding grounds for radical ideology extremists and create sanctuaries for terrorists, criminals, and insurgents. Of the 177 countries in the world, 38 have been defined as failed states, with 22 of those being in Africa.[25]

These failed states, along with other politically unstable nations, form an interconnected chain known as the 'arc of instability' (see Figure 1). This is a swath of territory covering most of western and northern South America, the Caribbean, most of Africa, the Middle East, and Central and Southeast Asia.[26] This area also includes the Caliphate claimed by Islamic extremists. A vast majority of the nations in the arc of instability border against the sea, and this area encompasses six sea lines of communication chokepoints: the Panama Canal, Bosporus and Dardanelles Straits, Suez Canal, Bab el Mandeb, Strait of Hormuz, and Strait of Malacca.[27] Since the end of the Cold War, 95 percent of all U.S. military overseas interventions have occurred within the arc of instability.[28] To combat future challenges to its national security, the United States requires a military force that is expeditionary and can operate effectively across the range of military operations.

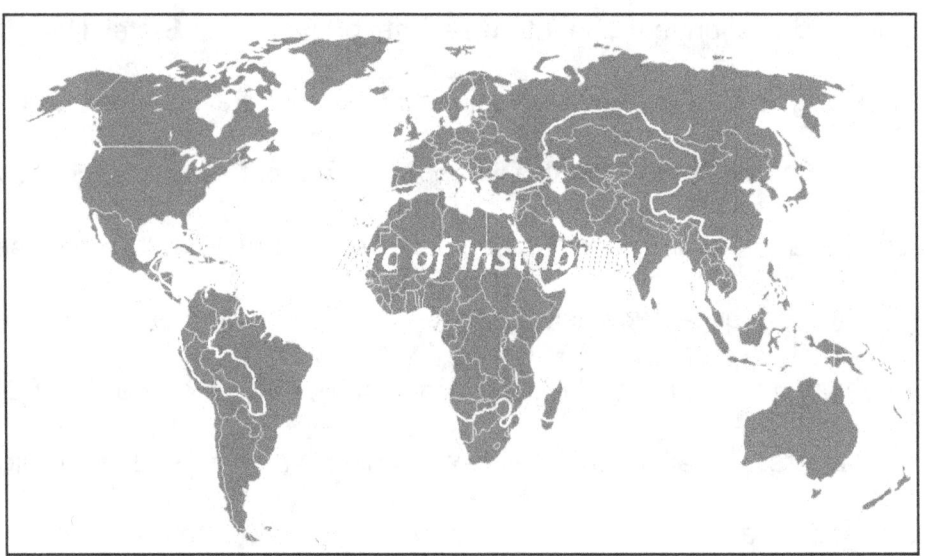

Figure 1: Arc of Instability *

Post Cold War Army

At the end of the Cold War the United States Army was the premier army of the world. For 40 years, the U.S. Army had organized, equipped, and trained itself to

8

confront the Soviet Union's mechanized army on the plains of Europe. For 40 years it had refined its doctrine, tactics, and techniques to be able to defeat the numerically superior Soviet war machine. The U.S. Army was extremely good at what it did and validated its conventional superiority during the Gulf War in 1991, when it rolled across the deserts of Saudi Arabia and Kuwait and defeated the Iraqi Army—driving it out of Kuwait and back into Iraq—within 100 hours.[29] The U.S. Army had no rival when it came to high intensity land warfare.

After the Gulf War, the United States military forces were downsized. With the Soviet Union gone, there were no peer competitors in conventional warfare on the horizon. The Army looked towards technology to offset its shrinking force and to maintain its battlefield dominance. A so called 'revolution in military affairs' got underway to transform the Army into a high-tech organization.[30] Satellites, computers, and other technological advancements offered improved communications, better command and control, more effective precision guided munitions, and robust intelligence collection capabilities.[31] Technology would improve the individual soldier's and commander's situational awareness and aid in the speed of decision making. Digital Technology led the Army's initiative with Force XXI, which aimed to increase the lethality, survivability, and operational tempo of ground forces.[32] At the same time, the Army began experimenting with its force structure to find the right mix of heavy and light units to form the optimum force for future conflicts.

The Army was superior to Cold War type opponents but had to be able to dominate across the full range of military operations for the 21st Century to best contribute to the future security of the Nation. The Army undertook an ambitious initiative to transform the static, Division-centric, armor heavy organization of the Cold War era into an agile, Brigade Combat Team-centric, modular organization. The 'modular army' concept utilizes brigades as the basic building blocks to tailor a specific task organized force to fulfill the needs of combatant commanders.[33] Multifunctional modules of combined arms, strike, aviation, reconnaissance and surveillance, protection, and sustainment are pieced together to form a deployable, self-sufficient force.[34] This broke the mold of the 'one-size-fits-all' Army. Divisions can now be comprised of anywhere from one to five maneuver brigades with accompanying support brigade modules. Modularization is intended to enable the Army to meet the demands of the contemporary operational environment with a lethal force that is expeditionary in nature.[35]

The Quadrennial Defense Review of 2001 focused heavily on the transformation of the U.S. military to meet the strategic needs of the 21st century. In particular, it called for reorienting the U.S. military global posture, stating that the "concentration of forces in Western Europe and Northeast Asia was inadequate for the new strategic environment."[36] The U.S. military presence in Europe went from a Cold War high of approximately 250,000 troops to a strength of 40,000 troops; and the strength of U.S. military forces in Korea went from 50,000 in 1989 to roughly 28,000 by 2009.[37] The re-posturing of forces enabled the Army to deploy forces to Operations Iraqi Freedom and Enduring Freedom while maintaining a minimum of a one-to-one deployment to dwell time ratio for most active duty soldiers. It also enabled the Army to focus on shifting personnel and units for its modularization program.

Operations in Iraq and Afghanistan revealed the limitations of new technologies and emerging military capabilities and the problems associated with building a military force over reliant on technology. The Army's 'revolution in military affairs' transformation concept focused on winning wars quickly and at low cost, believing that "surveillance, communications, and information technologies would improve battlespace knowledge, eliminate surprise, and permit full spectrum dominance through precision-strike capabilities."[38] This concept neglected the political, cultural, and psychological context of war and proved ineffective in a counterinsurgency campaign with a fluid and illusive enemy.[39] To address this issue the Army's Training and Doctrine Command embarked on a new phase of evolutionary transformation known as 'Operational Adaptability'.[40]

Operational Adaptability changes the Army's conceptual focus from major combat operations to employing full spectrum operations in uncertain and complex environments.[41] This concept requires leaders to focus on the enemy—continuously applying critical thinking to the situation, policies, and objectives—and to make rapid decisions while accepting risk in ambiguous operating environments.[42] This concept capitalizes on the Army's modularization program to provide expeditionary, task organized forces that can rapidly deploy anywhere in the world on short notice, for extended periods of time.[43] This capstone concept calls for the Army of the future to make full use of sealift capabilities to conduct shaping and forcible entry operations.[44] It also calls for the Army to develop sea-basing means to aid in overcoming enemy anti-access and area denial capabilities and to achieve surprise by conducting offensive operations from unexpected locations.[45]

But this concept takes the Army further away from being able to execute its primary mission of fighting and winning the Nation's land wars. The conventional warfighting capability that the Army developed during the Cold War has been significantly degraded during its repeated efforts at transformation and its focus on counterinsurgency operations continues to atrophy its combined arms capability along with other critical warfighting functions. The 2010 Quadrennial Defense Review exacerbates this issue by directing the Army to convert another heavy brigade combat team (and possibly even more heavy armor units) to a lighter Stryker brigade configuration and directs the focus of warfighting skills to be on counterinsurgency and stability operations.[46] The agile, expeditionary, task organized, force in readiness that the Army is attempting to transform into already exists—the United States Marine Corps.

## A Force in Readiness

The Marine Corps is the United States' force in readiness. It has been mandated by Congress to be "the most ready when the Nation is…least ready."[47] It is not intended to be a second land army.[48] Instead, its primary mission is to train, organize, and equip landing forces for amphibious operations and subsequent combat operations ashore and provide a balanced ground-air task force capable of suppressing and containing international disturbances short of large scale war.[49] The Marine Corps, in conjunction with the Navy, is tasked to develop amphibious doctrine and to maintain an amphibious forcible entry capability.[50]

The Marine Corps' principle organization construct is based on the Marine Air Ground Task Force (MAGTF) concept, where ground, aviation, and logistic units all fall directly under one commander to thoroughly integrate their combined combat capabilities into one very powerful and versatile force. MAGTFs are scalable and task organized to meet the operational needs of combatant commanders. There are three general MAGTFs which vary in size: the Marine Expeditionary Force (MEF), which is the largest; the Marine Expeditionary Brigade (MEB), and the Marine Expeditionary Unit (MEU), which is the smallest. In addition, the Marine Corps can create Special Purpose MAGTFs (SPMAGTF) which are composited in size and capabilities for specific missions with a defined scope and duration. The MAGTF's organic combined arms and combat service support assets provide a well-balanced, self-sufficient force in readiness capable of conducting missions across the range of military operations on short notice.[51]

In general, MAGTFs are expeditionary and can deploy either aboard ship or be flown to a crisis area. To enhance the expeditionary capability of the MAGTF, the Marine Corps has strategically prepositioned war reserves throughout the world, both afloat and ashore, giving the MAGTF the flexibility to link-up with weapons, vehicles, equipment, and combat service support assets at a forward location to reduce response time.[52]

The Marine Corps' preposition ashore program can support operations either independently or in combination with afloat assets.[53] Ashore programs are positioned near ports and airfields and may enable a faster response time than afloat programs. The Marine Corps has two ashore program sites, one in Norway and one in Kuwait.[54] The primary focus of the Marine Corps Prepositioning Program-Norway is for humanitarian assistance and disaster relief and is organized around equipping a MEB, which is the basic building block for large MAGTF operations.[55] In Kuwait, the MEU

Augmentation Program consists of equipment and supplies specific to the U.S. Central Command Theater of Operation and can augment a MEU-size force.[56]

The Marine Corps' preposition afloat program is a key component in the United States global maritime expeditionary strategy and consists of three Maritime Prepositioning Ships (MPS) Squadrons, each comprised of four to seven commercial ships.[57] These squadrons are strategically located throughout the world to provide overlapping coverage so that at least one squadron can be at a desired location within seven days of notification.[58] Each MPS Squadron contains a preponderance of the equipment and supplies to support a MEB.[59] MPS Squadrons do not have forcible entry capability and require a permissive environment for employment.[60]

The Marine Corps executes its mission of being the Nation's force in readiness by having one MEF on the west coast of the United States, a second MEF on the east coast, and a third MEF permanently forward deployed in the Pacific Theater, primarily on Okinawa, Japan. In addition, the Marine Corps has MEUs continuously forward deployed aboard ships. The Marine Corps has a total of seven MEUs: three stationed on the east coast, three on the west coast, and one based in Okinawa, Japan.[61] At any given time there are a minimum of two MEUs deployed throughout the world, generally to troubled areas.[62] MEUs deploy in support of combatant commanders and often serve as the theater reserve. MEUs undergo an intense six-month training program with the Navy before deploying and are capable of conducting missions across the range of military operations, from humanitarian assistance to major combat operations, within six hours of mission notification.[63] MEUs can operate independently or serve as an enabling force for follow-on forces.[64] Because they are forward deployed aboard ship,

14

MEUs are a superb rapid response force and can often be the first on the scene in the event of a crisis.

Strategic Concept

In the 1950s, the U.S. Congress realized the vital need for the existence of a strong force in readiness that was versatile, fast-moving, and hard-hitting; that could provide for the security of the Nation and implement its strategic concepts and global responsibilities.[65] This force needed to be powerful enough to quell minor international disturbances and prevent the development of "potential large conflagrations by prompt and vigorous action during their incipient stages."[66] This force had to be highly mobile and combat ready at all times so it could be quickly positioned anywhere in the world in the event of a national crisis to hold a major conflict at bay until America's vast war machine could be mobilized.[67] Congress saw the Marine Corps, with its amphibious forcible entry capability, as the Nation's shock troops and authorized it an end strength of 400,000 Marines to accomplish the mission of being the Nation's strategic force in readiness.[68] With its forward posture and unique expeditionary capabilities, the Marine Corps remains the ideal military force for the current and future global strategic operating environment.

Amphibious forces play a vital role in U.S. national strategy and are essential for maintaining security of the global commons, strengthening and expanding alliances, and deterring and defeating threats to national security, both big and small. Within the last 20 years, U.S. amphibious forces have responded to more than 104 crises throughout the world; a crisis response rate that is more than twice the amount as during the Cold War.[69] The rapid and decisive intervention of amphibious forces prevented a vast majority of these crises from escalating into major international conflicts.  With the reduction of U.S. military forces permanently stationed overseas and the reluctance of foreign nations to allow U.S. forces on their soil or to transit their airspace, gaining access to future crisis locations may only be attainable via the sea, which places an even greater emphasis on maintaining security in the sea commons.

The increase in piracy has restricted freedom of movement on the high seas in several parts of the world, in particular off the coast of East Africa and in the Strait of Malacca, two major international commercial shipping areas.  Fearing capture by pirates, commercial vessels are either arming themselves and developing tactics to fight off pirates or are making long—very expensive—navigational detours to avoid pirate infested waters.[70]  Increased naval operations in troubled areas have had a significant impact on curtailing pirate activity and amphibious forces are playing an increasing role in this vital international effort.[71]

For example, elements of the 26th MEU were tasked to support counter-piracy operations in the fall of 2008 when pirates captured the Ukrainian Motor Vessel Faina off the coast of Somalia, which was carrying T-72 tanks and a large quantity of ammunitions and small arms.[72]  The 26th MEU also supported Combined Task Force 151 counter-piracy operations in January and February 2009 and was involved in the detainment of seven Somalia pirates.[73]  The 13th MEU performed counter-piracy operations with Combined Task Force 151 for three months in the spring of 2009 and was instrumental in the planning and execution of a multitude of counter-piracy operations to include the hostage situation with Captain Richard Phillip and the Motor Vessel Maersk Alabama which resulted in the death of two pirates and the capture of a third.[74]

Within a one year period, from August 2008 to September 2009, U.S. and other cooperative naval forces captured over 550 pirates and killed 11 more.[75] To further its resolve at combating this strategic problem, the Marine Corps has reinstituted its Maritime Interdiction Operation capability within its MEUs and will begin prosecuting offensive ship-boarding counter-piracy operations with organic visit, board, search, and seizure teams in 2010.[76] The versatility of Marine Corps amphibious forces plays an important role in retaining freedom of the seas and in developing international partnerships.

Strengthening and expanding international alliances and partnerships is essential for the United States to carry out its National Security Strategy of promoting democracy and to secure its vital national interests. The United States pursues this endeavor by providing diplomatic, economic, and military assistance to its allies, weak and failing states, and where possible, failed states. The Marine Corps supports the military realm of this strategic concept with a security cooperation program aimed at furthering U.S. national security interests and promoting U.S. values abroad.[77] The unique operating capabilities that amphibious forces offer make the Marine Corps ideally suited for executing security cooperation activities in a strategic operating environment where the political climate may restrict access and over flight of U.S. military forces.

The Marine Corps security cooperation program maximizes contributions to support security cooperation initiatives of the geographical combatant commanders and covers a wide variety of military-to-military training and education programs along with other comparable operational activities.[78] Within the last three years, the Marine Corps has conducted more than 160 security cooperation activities with foreign nations.[79]

These activities focused on building partner security capacity across the warfighting functions through multinational training exercises, security assistance, international armaments cooperation, and counter-narcotic assistance, just to highlight a few.[80] Despite a significant number of Marine forces participating in Operations Enduring Freedom and Iraqi Freedom, the Marine Corps has continued to conduct security cooperation activities with an increased emphasis in Africa.

Marine Corps security cooperation activities in Africa went from one or two a year in the early 2000s to 14 in 2009, and were conducted by both shore based and amphibious forces.[81] With 35 African countries bordering the sea—most of them being failed or failing states—amphibious forces provide the U.S. Africa Command Combatant Commander with the flexibility of conducting security cooperation activities without having to base units ashore. Initiatives such as the African Partnership Station are stand alone security cooperation programs that utilize amphibious ships to house U.S. and international personnel and to serve as training platforms.[82] Depending on the particular political climate of a country, the ships can either remain in the international maritime domain or pull into port, and the training of host nation military personnel can either take place ashore or on ship.[83] When the mission is complete, the ships, along with all security cooperation personnel depart the area leaving behind no permanent U.S. foot print. Forward deployed amphibious forces have demonstrated their ability to build enduring foreign relationships throughout the world. However, when the United States is unsuccessful at building harmonious relationships, amphibious forces serve equally well as deterrents to would be adversaries.

The United States can't make every state, group, or organization agree with its policies or conform to its way of thinking, but in the contemporary strategic environment the United States can effectively shape the choices of others. The lethality, versatility, and rapid response of forward deployed Naval expeditionary forces enforce the strategic concept of deterring a wide range of potential adversaries from taking action against the United States and its vital national interests. Deterrence is the key to enhancing security and preventing conflict and is based on credibility.[84] The United States' ability to project and sustain power ashore is its combat credibility. It is impossible to tell how many United States adversaries were deterred from taking action against the United States because Naval expeditionary forces were sitting off the coast of their country, but history clearly shows the strategic importance of amphibious forces and their ability to significantly influence land combat operations.

History has shown the enormous impact amphibious forces have in conflicts. During the Second World War, when the Germans began their offensive against the Russians on their eastern front, they left 35 full divisions to guard the coastal areas of Western, Northwestern, and Southwestern Europe; despite having recently destroyed nearly all of Britain's combat capabilities during fighting in France, where only personnel were able to be hastily extracted from Dunkirk without their implements of war.[85] More than 27 percent of the German combat forces were withheld from the German army's most ambitious endeavor to date because of the potential of amphibious forces striking somewhere along the vast stretch of European coastline.[86] Similarly, in 1944 the Germans had only positioned 10 percent of their combat divisions in Northern France to fend off the allied invasion on 6 June.[87] The other 25 percent of the German divisions that were not committed to the Russian front were drawn westward and southward to guard against possible invasions along those coastlines.[88]

In 1991 during the Gulf War, an amphibious demonstration off the coast of Kuwait by the 4th Marine Expeditionary Brigade effectively tied down six Iraqi Divisions—41,000 troops—to the Kuwaiti coastline and prevented their repositioning to the main battle area.[89] In order for the United States to deter future conflicts and adversaries, it must maintain a credible ability to project combat power ashore, which is best accomplished with a formidable amphibious forcible entry capability.

Future Amphibious Requirements

The ever changing global political climate indicates a future world full of uncertainty and conflict. To identify and prepare for the challenges of the future, one needs to examine the challenges of the past. Thucydides noted long ago that based on human nature "the events that happened in the past…will at some time or other…be repeated in the future."[90] Amphibious forces have played a significant role in major powers throughout history and have proven vital to the security of the United States for over a century. Even with modern technology and the invention of nuclear weapons, amphibious forces have been relied upon to fight conflicts and preserve the security of the United States, despite the efforts of top national political and military leaders to do away with them. In 1949, the Secretary of Defense and Chairman of the Joint Chiefs of Staff advised President Truman that amphibious operations were archaic and obsolete and that they would never be needed again.[91] Less than a year later, the United States Army and Marine Corps conducted a major amphibious assault at Inchon, which initiated U.S. offensive actions against the communists during the Korean War. The future was uncertain in 1949, and with the blurring of regular and irregular warfare it remains uncertain today.

Today's hybrid threats and failing states make the requirement for an amphibious forcible entry capability even more viable. The global proliferation of sophisticated anti-access weapons by state and non-state actors make the challenges of maintaining access to areas of strategic importance even more lethal; as demonstrated by Hezbollah employing C-802 anti-ship missiles against Israeli ships during the Lebanon crisis in 2006.[92] Even relatively small extremist organizations with low-tech weaponry operating with autonomy in a failed state can provide significant challenges and threats to United States military power. It is not difficult to render port facilities or coastlines unattainable to forces without an amphibious forcible entry capability. Future maritime concepts such as sea-basing allow amphibious forces to exploit the United States' command of the sea by being able to project forces ashore without relying on other nations to provide land bases, port facilities, or airfields. Other innovative operational concepts such as the Marine Corps 'operational maneuver from the sea' and 'ship-to-objective maneuver' utilize the sea as a maneuver area to come from beyond the horizon, bypassing area denial weapon systems, and surprising the enemy by attacking it where it is unexpected.[93]

Such operational concepts have proven quite effective in small-scale, limited-duration amphibious operations. In 1995, amphibious forces of the 24th MEU rescued Air Force pilot Captain Scott O'Grady after he was shot down over Bosnia. In 2001, amphibious forces linked up in the North Arabian Sea and brought together two Marine Expeditionary Units under Task Force 58 and initiated U.S. offensive combat operations in Afghanistan several hundred miles inland.  And in 2006, amphibious forces in the Mediterranean Sea, which included the 24th MEU, conducted noncombatant evacuation operations in Lebanon and evacuated thousands of U.S. and allied nation diplomats and citizens when hostilities erupted throughout the country.  The United States routinely executes small-scale amphibious operations, demonstrating their effectiveness and versatility, and establishing U.S. credibility in this domain of warfare.  However, conducting large-scale amphibious operations is problematic.

The credibility of the United States to conduct large-scale amphibious forcible entry operations is limited by its number of amphibious ships.  At the end of the Second World War, more than 37 percent of the ships in the U.S. Navy were amphibious and could land 13 divisions across the beach without reliance on forward land bases.[94]  In 1981, the U.S. Navy had enough amphibious ships to transport 4.0 MEBs, which is one entire MEF plus another MEB, roughly 53,240 Marines and their equipment (nearly half of the Marine Corps operating forces).[95]  Today, merely 10 percent of the U.S. Navy's ships are amphibious and they can't even land a single division across the beach.  The 32 amphibious ships the U.S. Navy possesses can transport a little less than 2.0 MEBs personnel and only a portion of their equipment.[96]  In 2009, both the Chief of Naval Operations and the Commandant of the Marine Corps agreed the requirement for shipping to support a 2.0 MEB lift of personnel and equipment is 38 total amphibious assault ships.[97]  However, the 2010 Quadrennial Defense Review compounds the shortage of amphibious lift capability by calling for a reduction of amphibious ships to between 29 and 31.[98]

Doctrinally, the MEF is the MAGTF stipulated in combatant commanders' war plans to fight major combat operations, which is a 3.0 MEB force.[99] Due to the lack of amphibious shipping, the Marine Corps' plan for providing a 3.0 MEB force is to augment the amphibious 2.0 MEB forcible entry assault echelon force with a 1.0 MEB assault follow-on echelon force which will fall in on a Maritime Preposition Force (MPF) gear set.[100] However, the use of MPF assets requires a benign environment for employment. This plan makes the assumption that port facilities and airfields will be available for the assault follow-on force to use. Given today's strategic operating environment, this is an extremely risky assumption to make. Increasing the number of amphibious ships to provide a 3.0 MEB forcible entry capability would not only meet the requirements of combatant commanders' war plans, but would also give Naval Forces the ability to meet other needs of the combatant commanders in carrying out the national strategy.

Combatant commanders realize the enormous utility of amphibious forces. Their cumulative requests for persistent forward deployed amphibious forces for 2010 equates to four MEUs and two smaller, task-organized amphibious SPMAGTFs.[101] These requests double the amount of amphibious forces utilized in the previous year. In addition to having amphibious forces serve as the theater reserve, combatant commanders desire to incorporate amphibious forces into security cooperation initiatives. The versatility and independent nature of amphibious forces have greatly aided in bringing stability to volatile regions and spreading American values and good will to troubled areas in South America, Africa, and other parts of the world. Amphibious forces are at a premium, and additional amphibious shipping will help pave the way for meeting the initiatives and operational needs of combatant commanders.

## Conclusion

To continue to expand its global influence, implement its National Security Strategy, and combat future threats in a world that is evolving and constantly changing, the United States needs to capitalize on a military force that has proven itself effective in the current strategic operating environment and expound upon its capabilities to meet the uncertain challenges of the future. The Marine Corps, with its expeditionary nature and unique forward deployed amphibious capability, has proven itself extremely effective as the Nation's strategic force in readiness.

Secretary of Defense Robert M. Gates is absolutely correct when he calls for a need to strike the right balance in military forces to be able to combat current and future threats and implement the National Security Strategy of the United States.[102] However, transforming the Army into a light expeditionary force isn't the answer. There are still adversarial states with formidable military forces that require the United States to maintain a strong conventional Army that can defeat enemies in major land conflicts and win the Nation's wars. Expanding upon the Nation's amphibious capabilities and procuring the means to fully implement innovative operational concepts that exploit the United States' command of the seas is a step in the right direction of striking the right balance.

The Marine Corps—America's shock troops—coupled with the Navy's amphibious ships enables the United States to rapidly project power around the world, protect its global vital national interests, and enhance global stability. The United States Marine Corps is the ideal military force for a globally engaged super power.

Endnotes

[1] Harry S. Truman, *National Security Council Paper: NSC 68* (Washington, DC: The White House, April 7, 1950), sect. VI, subpar. a.

[2] Stephen Daggett and Amy Belasco, *Defense Budget for FY2003: Data Summary*, CRS-RL31349 (Washington, DC: Library of Congress, Congressional Research Service, March 29, 2002), 16, http://fpc.state.gov/documents/ organization/9665.pdf (accessed November 7, 2009).

[3] "U.S. Nuclear Weapons Enduring Stockpile," last changed August 31, 2007, http://nuclearweaponarchive.org/Usa/Weapons/Wpngall.html (accessed November 6, 2009); and Amy F. Woolf, *Nuclear Weapons in the Former Soviet Union: Location, Command, and Control*, CRS-91144 (Washington, DC: Library of Congress, Congressional Research Service, November 27, 1996), http://www.fas.org/spp/starwars/crs/91-144.htm (accessed November 6, 2009).

[4] Anne Leland and Mari-Jana Oboroceanu, *American War and Military Operations Casualties: List and Statistics*, CRS-RL32492 (Washington, DC: Library of Congress, Congressional Research Service, September 15, 2009), 3, http://www.fas.org/sgp/crs/ natsec/RL32492.pdf (accessed November 6, 2009).

[5] George W. Bush, *The National Security Strategy of the United States of America* (Washington, DC: The White House, March 2006), ii.

[6] Ibid., 1.

[7] Ibid.

[8] Robert M. Gates, *National Defense Strategy* (Washington, DC: U.S. Department of Defense, June 2008), 6.

[9] Ibid., 6, 11-16.

[10] Data points in this paragraph obtained from MajGen Robert E. Schmidle, "Marine Corps Underscores Nation's Need for Ships," brief to Congressional Ship Building Caucus, March 24, 2009, http://www.taylor.house.gov/shipbuildingcaucus/index.php?options=com_content&task= view&id=22&Itemid=1 (accessed December 27, 2009).

[11] Ibid.

[12] Richard Allard et al., *High Fidelity Simulations of Littoral Environments* (Arlington, VA: Office of Naval Research, June 2002), 1, http://www.dtic.mil/cgi-bin/GetTRDoc?AD= ADA419564&Location=U2&doc= GetTRDoc.pdf (accessed December 27, 2009).

[13] U.S. Marine Corps, *Amphibious Operations in the 21st Century* (Quantico, VA: Marine Corps Combat Development Command, March 18, 2009), 2.

[14] Gerry J. Gilmore, "U.S.,Turkey Announce Operation Iraqi Freedom Support Agreement," *American Forces Press Service* (April 2, 2003), http://www.defense.gov/news/ newsarticle.aspx?id=29175 (accessed December 29, 2009).

[15] Michele Flournoy and Shawn Brimley, "The Contested Commons," *Proceeding*, Vol. 135 (July 2009), http://www.usni.org/magazines/proceedings/story.asp?STORY_ID=1950 (accessed November 1, 2009).

[16] Robert S. Ross, "China's Naval Nationalism: Sources, Prospects, and the U.S. Response," *International Security*, vol. 34, iss.2 (Fall 2009): 46.

[17] Massimo Annati, "Part 1: The Threat the Iranian Navy and the 'Naval Pasdaran': Asymmetric Warfare Mastered by the Gatekeepers of the Gulf," *Naval Forces*, vol. 30 (2009): 28.

[18] Deborah Stead, "Hedging Bets on the High Seas," *Business Week* (April 27, 2009): 10.

[19] Max Boot, *War Made New: Technology, Warfare, and the Course of History, 1500 to Today* (New York: Random House, 2006), 472.

[20] Frank G. Hoffman, "Hybrid Warfare and Challenges," *Joint Forces Quarterly*, (1st Quarter 2009): 37.

[21] Ibid.

[22] U.S. Department of Defense, *Irregular Warfare (IW), Joint Operating Concept (JOC), Version 1.0* (Washington, DC: U.S. Department of Defense, September 11, 2007), 11.

[23] Nathen Freier, "The Defense Identity Crisis: It's a Hybrid World," *Parameters* (Autumn 2009): 85.

[24] Stephen D. Krasner and Carlos Pascual, "Addressing State Failure," *Foreign Affairs*, vol. 84, no. 4 (July/August 2005): 153.

[25] Fund for Peace, "Failed State Index 2009," http://www.fundforpeace.org/web/index.php?option=com_content&task=view&id=391&Itemid=549 (accessed December 22, 2009).

[26] Thomas P.M. Barnett, *Statement to Seapower and Expeditionary Forces Subcommittee, House Armed Services Committee, United States Congress*, (Washington, DC: U.S. Congress, March 26, 2009), 5, http://armedservices.house.gov/pdfs/SPEF032609/Barnett_Testimony 032609.pdf (accessed December 29, 2009).

[27] Ibid.

[28] Ibid.

[29] U.S. Department of Defense, *Conduct of Persian Gulf War: Final Report to Congress* (Washington, DC: U.S. Department of Defense, April 2002), 18,19, http://ndu.edu/library/epubs/cpgw.pdf (accessed December 29, 2009).

[30] U.S. Department of the Army, *The Army Capstone Concept: Operational Adaptability: Operating under Conditions of Uncertainty and Complexity in an Era of Persistent Conflict 2016-2028*, TRADOC Pam 525-3-0 (Washington, DC: U.S. Department of the Army, December 21, 2009), 6.

[31] Ibid.

[32] Mark Hanna, "Task Force XXI: The Army's Digital Experiment," *Strategic Forum*, no. 119 (July 1997), http://www.ndu.edu/inss/Strforum/SF119/forum119.html#top (accessed December 29, 2009).

[33] John A. Bonin and Telford E. Crisco, "The Modular Army," *Military Review* (March-April 2004): 27.

[34] Ibid.

[35] Ibid., 25.

[36] U.S. Department of Defense, *Quadrennial Defense Review Report: 2001* (Washington, DC: U.S. Department of Defense, September 30, 2001), 25.

[37] Amy K. Holmes, "Redeployment Reconsiderations: Rumsfeld, Gates, and the U.S. Presence in Germany," *American Institute for Contemporary German Studies* (May 16, 2008), http://www.aicgs.org/documents/advisor/holmes0508.pdf (accessed December 29, 2009); and Larry A. Niksch, *Korea-U.S. Relations: Issues for Congress*, CRS-RL33567 (Washington, DC: Library of Congress, Congressional Research Services, updated April 28, 2008), 1, http://fpc.state.gov/documents/organization/105198.pdf (accessed December 29, 2009).

[38] U.S. Department of the Army, *The Army Capstone Concept, Operational Adaptability*, 6.

[39] Ibid.

[40] Ibid., 1.

[41] Ibid., 1.

[42] Ibid., 16.

[43] Ibid., 37.

[44] Ibid., 26.

[45] Ibid., 27.

[46] U.S. Department of Defense, *Quadrennial Defense Review Report: 2010* (Washington, DC: U.S. Department of Defense, February 2010), 24.

[47] U.S. Congress, *U.S. Code Congressional and Administrative News: Legislative History Commentaries*, 82nd Congress, 2nd Session, vol. 2 (Brooklyn, NY: Edward Thompson Co., 1953), 1763.

[48] U.S. Department of Defense, *Functions of the Department of Defense and Its Major Components*, DOD Directive 5100.1 (Washington, DC: U.S. Department of Defense, August 1, 2002), 18.

[49] Ibid.; and U.S. Congress, *U.S. Code Congressional and Administrative News*, 1763.

[50] U.S. Department of Defense, *Functions of the Department of Defense*, 18.

[51] U.S. Marine Corps, *Expeditionary Operations*, MCDP 3 (Quantico, VA: Marine Corps Combat Development Command, April 1998), 69.

[52] U.S. Marine Corps, *Marine Corps Prepositioning Road Map 2025: Shaping Global Prepositioning* (Quantico, VA: Marine Corps Combat Development Command, July 2009), 8.

[53] Ibid.

[54] Ibid.

[55] Ibid.

[56] Ibid.

[57] Ibid., 7.

[58] Ibid., 7.

[59] Ibid., 7.

[60] Ibid., 18

[61] U.S. Marine Corps, *U.S. Marine Corps Concepts & Programs 2009* (Quantico, VA: Marine Corps Combat Development Command, 2009), 49, 52, 54.

[62] Ibid., 32.

[63] Ibid., 38, 39.

[64] Ibid., 39.

[65] U.S. Congress, *U.S. Code Congressional and Administrative News*, 1757, 1758.

[66] Ibid., 1757, 1758.

[67] Ibid., 1757, 1758.

[68] Ibid., 1757.

[69] U.S. Marine Corps, *Amphibious Operations in the 21st Century*, 3, 4.

[70] Lauren Caldwell, "Pirate Attacks Off Africa Less Successful, Officials Say," July 7, 2009, http://www.ameerica.gov/st/peacesec-english/2009/July/20090707105709ALllewdlaCO.4344446.html (accessed December 29, 2009).

[71] Lauren Ploch et al., *Piracy off the Horn of Africa*, CRS-R40528 (Washington, DC: Library of Congress, Congressional Research Service, April 24, 2009), 16, http://italy.usembassy.gov/pdf/other/R40528.pdf (accessed December 30, 2009).

[72] Ibid.  The author was the Commanding Officer of Battalion Landing Team 2/6 (the ground combat element for the 26th MEU) and the battalion provided an 8-man sniper team and a Russian linguist to support this counter-piracy operation.

[73] Brian Goodwin, "San Antonio Key to Counterpiracy Mission," January 17, 2009, http://www.navy.mil/Search/display.asp?story_id=41844 (accessed December 30, 2009).  The author was the Commanding Officer of Battalion Landing Team 2/6 (the ground combat element for the 26th MEU) and the battalion provided a reinforced rifle platoon to provide detainee security for CTF-151 aboard USS San Antonio.

[74] 13th Marine Expeditionary Unit Website, "13th MEU Marines and Sailors come home after seven month deployment," July 30, 2009, http://13thmeu.blogspot.com/2009/07/13th-meu-marines-and-sailors-come-home.html (accessed December 31, 2009).

[75] Brianna K. Dandridge, "Pirate Attacks on Rise off Somalia Coast," September 19, 2009, http://www.centcom.mil/en/press-release/pirate-attacks-on-rise-off-somalia-coast.html (accessed December 30, 2009).

[76] U.S. Marine Corps, *United States Marine Corps Service Campaign Plan 2009-2015* (Washington, DC: Headquarters U.S. Marine Corps, December 9, 2009), 13.

[77] U.S. Marine Corps, *USMC Security Cooperation*, MCO 5710.6A (Washington, DC: Headquarters U.S. Marine Corps, March 24, 2006), 2, http://www.marines.mil/news/publications/Documents/MCO%205710.6A.pdf (accessed January 1, 2010).

[78] Ibid.

[79] LtCol R. R. Scott, *Security Force Assistance Information Paper: Security Force Assistance Related Deployments/Exercises 2007-2009* (Washington, DC: Headquarters U.S. Marine Corps, Plans, Policy & Operations Division, no date), 1; author received document from LtCol R.R. Scott upon request on December 21, 2009.

[80] Ibid.

[81] Ibid.

[82] Rear Admiral William Loeffler, "Africa Partnership Station and Maritime Capacity Building in Africa," U.S. Department of State, Foreign Press Center Brief, March 26, 2009, http://fpc.sate.gov/121013.htm (accessed January 1, 2010).

[83] Ibid.

[84] Robert M. Gates, *National Defense Strategy*, 11.

[85] B.H. Liddell Hart, "Marines and Strategy," *Marine Corps Gazette* (July 1960): 11.

[86] Ibid., 12.

[87] Ibid., 12.

[88] Ibid., 12.

[89] P. Antill, "Gulf War – Coalition Amphibious Operations," February 26, 2003, *Military History Encyclopedia on the Web*, http://historyofwar.org/articles/wars_gulf_amphibious.html (accessed January 1, 2010).

[90] Thucydides, *The History of the Peloponnesian War*, trans. by Rex Warner (London: Penguin Books, 1954), 48.

[91] Robert D. Heinl, *Victory at High Tide: The Inchon-Seoul Campaign* (Philadelphia, PA: Lippincott Company, 1968), 3.

[92] U.S. Marine Corps, *Amphibious Operations in the 21st Century*, 22, 23.

[93] U.S. Marine Corps, *Operational Maneuver from the Sea* (Quantico, VA: Marine Corps Combat Development Command, January 4, 1994), 6; and U.S. Marine Corps, *Ship to Objective Maneuver* (Quantico, VA: Marine Corps Combat Development Command, July 25, 1997), II-3, II-9.

[94] U.S. Department of the Navy, "U.S. Navy Active Ship Levels," *Naval Historical Center Website*, http://www.history.navy.mil/branches/org9-4.htm#1938 (accessed November 7, 2009).

[95] Ronald O'Rourke, *Navy LPD-17 Amphibious Ship Procurement: Background, Issues, and Options for Congress*, CRS-RL34476 (Washington, DC: Library of Congress, Congressional Research Services, June 4, 2009), 5, http://fas.org/sgp/crs/weapons/RL34476.pdf (accessed January 2, 2010).

[96] Ibid., 1, 4.

[97] Ibid., 1.

[98] U.S. Department of Defense, *Quadrennial Defense Review Report: 2010*, 46.

[99] U.S. Department of the Navy, *Report to Congress on Naval Amphibious Force Structure* (Washington, DC: U.S. Department of the Navy, December 2008), 3.

[100] Ibid., 4.

[101] U.S. Marine Corps, *Amphibious Operations in the 21st Century*, 4.

[102] Robert M. Gates, "The National Defense Strategy: Striking the Right Balance," *Joint Forces Quarterly*, iss. 52 (1st Quarter 2009): 2.

www.ingramcontent.com/pod-product-compliance
Lightning Source LLC
Chambersburg PA
CBHW080742290526
45790CB00008B/3285